COSMIC CLASH
OF TH

T0011664

ZEUS

VS

RA

by Lydia Lukidis

CAPSTONE PRESS
a capstone imprint

Published by Capstone Press, an imprint of Capstone
1710 Roe Crest Drive, North Mankato, Minnesota 56003
capstonepub.com

Library of Congress Cataloging-in-Publication Data is
available on the Library of Congress website.
ISBN: 9781666343823 (hardcover)
ISBN: 9781666343847 (paperback)
ISBN: 9781666343854 (ebook PDF)

Summary:
It's a battle of the leader of gods versus the god of the sun. The Greek
god Zeus controls the skies and can shape-shift as he wishes. With his
connection to the sun, the Egyptian god Ra provides life, warmth, and
growth. If these two gods were to go head-to-head, who would come
out on top?

Editorial Credits
Editor: Julie Gassman; Designer: Heidi Thompson; Media Researchers:
Jo Miller and Pam Mitsakos; Production Specialist: Tori Abraham

Image Credits
Alamy: De Luan, 15, FOST, 24, The Picture Art Collection, 20; Getty
Images: GregSm, 17, Print Collector, 9, stigalenas, 29, ZU_09, 7;
Shutterstock: Aerial-motion, 23, Artem Tkachuk, 19, BlackMac, Cover
(Top), Breaking The Walls, 21, Esteban De Armas, 4, Gilmanshin, 27
(Left), Giorgos Ntentis, 10, Guido Vermeulen-Perdaen, 22, klyaksun,
5, Nomad_Soul, 27 (Right), SandraSWC, 28, siloto, Cover (Bottom),
Stellar_bones, 25, Vladimir Zadvinskii, 12, Zwiebackesser, 11

All internet sites appearing in back matter were available and accurate
when this book was sent to press.

TABLE OF CONTENTS

Words in **bold** are in the glossary.

TWO MIGHTY GODS

CRACK! Lightning rips through the sky. *BOOM!* Thunder rumbles through the air.

Looks like Zeus is in a bad mood again. As the god of the sky, he controls the weather. But he does so much more.

Zeus is the main **deity** in the ancient Greek religion. Plus, he leads the **Olympian** gods. His personality is larger than life. He can be charming, but watch out! You don't want to get on his bad side. Zeus is known for his terrible temper. It's either his way or the highway.

Zeus

Can anyone compete against the almighty Zeus? The most powerful god in Egypt can. He's the god of the sun and creation, among many other things. His name is Ra.

Ra takes on different forms. He usually has the head of a falcon and the body of a man. A round sun disk and a cobra rest on his head. The cobra is a symbol of royalty.

Ra

Who is more powerful? Who has more abilities? Gods Zeus and Ra will have to battle it out. The duel is on!

HOW DID THEY GET HERE?

Zeus's parents were the Greek **Titans** Cronus and Rhea. They ruled the ancient world. Cronus didn't exactly win the father of the year award.

One day, an **oracle** warned Cronus that one of his sons would defeat him. Cronus got nervous. Then he did something shocking. One by one, he ate his first five children. Down went Hestia, Demeter, Hera, Hades, and Poseidon.

Once Rhea realized what was happening, she saved their youngest child, Zeus. After giving birth to Zeus, she handed Cronus a rock wrapped in blankets. Cronus assumed it was Zeus and swallowed the rock. Rhea shipped baby Zeus off to a cave on the island of Crete. He grew up there.

Rhea saved Zeus from his father by giving Cronus a wrapped rock, which the god swallowed.

At the beginning of time, nothing existed. The world was a sea of **chaos** and darkness. Swirling **primeval** waters circled Earth. Ra sprang forth from those waters.

Most myths say the all-powerful Ra created himself. He didn't have parents. In fact, he already existed in those ancient waters. Then one day, poof! An island rose from the waters. It was the first dry land on Earth. Ra arose with it.

Some believe Ra later took on human form. At that point, he became the **pharaoh**.

Night and Day

A famous Egyptian myth describes Ra traveling across the sky in a boat during the day. He lights up the sky, creating daytime. Then each night, he travels through the **underworld** in another boat. The world then experiences nighttime.

Ra sometimes has a ram's head when he is shown traveling through the underworld.

MIND-BOGGLING STRENGTHS

What's Zeus's most famous strength? It is probably his collection of lightning bolts. These bolts are symbols of his power. He can use them anytime he needs. His winged horse, Pegasus, carries them, and an eagle retrieves them.

Pegasus

Zeus's eagle, which brought his arrows to him, was named Aetos Dios.

With these lightning bolts, Zeus controls the world. He often uses them as weapons. Those who dare question him pay the price.

Just ask poor old Asclepius. Asclepius was the god of medicine. His healing powers became so strong that he raised people from the dead. But Zeus didn't like anyone becoming as powerful as him. Then, *BAM!* He zapped Asclepius with his lightning bolts. That took care of that.

Ra's biggest strength lies in his connection with the sun. In fact, ancient Egyptians believed he *was* the sun himself. His role was to give life to his people and all creatures through the sun's rays. The sun provided life, warmth, and growth.

Ra is nearly always shown with a sun disk on his head. It symbolizes his connection to the sun.

The sun was also important for plants and crops. They need the sun to grow. Keep in mind, the Egyptians relied on farming. They grew and harvested crops to survive.

As the sun, Ra can also help change the seasons. Ancient Egyptians believed Ra directed the Nile River to flood each year. This flooding was the first of three seasons, each impacted by Ra.

The Three Seasons

Ancient Egypt's three seasons were organized around farming. First, heavy rainfalls flooded the Nile. Then, the floodwaters left a thick, rich mud. Farmers planted their crops. The season of harvest followed, and farmers also collected seeds to plant the next year. As the sun, Ra helped usher in these seasons.

Zeus is one sly guy. For example, he came up with a sneaky plan to defeat his father. He gave Cronus a poison. It made him vomit. As the puke spilled out, Zeus freed his five siblings. They had been stuck inside their father's belly ever since he swallowed them.

Zeus is also a brave warrior. When his parents tried to beat the Olympian gods, he wasn't having it. He led the Olympians to a 10-year battle and won.

Zeus fought in many other battles. He even fought against the Giants. He led his gods to victory that time as well. His abilities as a warrior make him dangerous.

FACT

Zeus and his brothers divided the world among themselves. Zeus took charge of the sky and air. Poseidon took control of the sea. Hades took control of the underworld.

After freeing his siblings, Zeus led the gods in a
battle against the Titans.

Ra also has another strength up his sleeve. It's his secret name. When someone says this secret name out loud, they can do or be anything they want. It's so powerful that Ra must hide it from others, and no one knows it.

Ra can also multitask. In a nutshell, he's in charge of everything in the Egyptian world. He controls the sky, Earth, and the underworld.

Although he's the main god, he also **merges** with other gods. For example, when Ra is in the underworld, he joins with Osiris, the god of the dead. When he's in the sky, he blends with Shu, the god of the air and sky. Ra takes on many roles. He can pretty much do whatever he wants, whenever he wants.

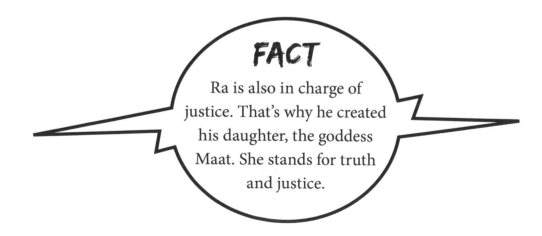

FACT

Ra is also in charge of justice. That's why he created his daughter, the goddess Maat. She stands for truth and justice.

The Egyptian god of the dead, Osiris, was also the god of farming. This is why his skin is green.

AWESOME SUPERPOWERS

Both gods are **immortal** and have different superpowers. For one, Zeus can control the weather. When he's in a good mood, Zeus creates nice weather. But when he's in a bad mood, steer clear! He may cause strong winds, rain, and violent storms. In one myth, he got annoyed with **mortals**. So he caused a gigantic flood that wiped them all out.

Zeus also has the power to **shape-shift** into anything he wants. For example, he once transformed himself into a beautiful swan. Why, you may wonder? It was to romance Princess Leda. When an eagle chased the swan, Leda felt bad for it. She took care of it and gave it her attention. Little did she know, the swan was Zeus!

The story of Princess Leda and the swan has inspired many pieces of art.

What's Ra's most awesome superpower? It's his ability to be the ultimate creator. Not only did he create himself, but he also created his own children. He simply breathed life into them. Suddenly, Tefnut and Shu sprang forth.

Tefnut (left) and Shu

The Eye of Ra sees everything. It is a symbol
of power and royal authority.

Ra also created mortals. At the beginning of time,
he sent his children to start forming the world. They
were gone a long time. Ra began to worry, so he pulled
out one of his eyes. He sent that eye, called the Eye of
Ra, to search for his children. When the eye brought
them back, Ra was grateful and shed tears of joy. These
tears fell on the ground. They changed themselves into
men and women.

Believe it or not, Zeus and Ra have a few things in common. Both are the main gods of their **pantheons**. Zeus leads the Greeks, and Ra leads the Egyptians. Many see them as father figures. In fact, they call Zeus the father of both gods and men. They call Ra the king and father of the king.

Both Zeus and Ra are control freaks. They need to be the most powerful. And they need to be in charge of everything.

King Ramesses III's (left) name showed the belief that Ra (right) was his father. *Ramesses* means "Ra is the one who bore him."

People from all over the world used to honor Zeus and Ra. The Greeks created the Olympic Games to honor Zeus. The games began as a festival in Olympia. They continue around the world today. Ancient Egyptians believed that most of their gods and pharaohs were related to Ra. The pharaohs built sun temples to honor Ra.

Ancient Greeks built the Temple of Olympian Zeus in Athens in the god's honor. Today just 15 columns of the temple remain standing.

GODLY ISSUES

Even though both gods are powerful, they aren't perfect. They have their fair share of issues.

Zeus's main weakness can be summed up in one word: women. He falls in love easily and can't remain loyal. His first wife was the Titan Metis, but that didn't last long. He went on to marry and date many goddesses and mortal women. He eventually married his own sister, Hera. Yet he continued to date other women.

Hera

Zeus also has a bad temper. If someone upsets him, he zaps them with his lightning bolt. He also bullies others. The Titan Prometheus is a great example. When Prometheus didn't follow Zeus's orders, Zeus told an eagle to eat his liver. And it gets worse. He made Prometheus's liver heal every night. That way, the eagle could eat it all over again the next day.

Zeus's eagle was both his messenger and pet.

Ra's main issue is the fact that he's an **egomaniac**. The world pretty much revolves around him and his desires. If he doesn't get what he wants, he throws temper tantrums. He can even be violent.

In one myth, Ra was growing old, and humans were tired of him. They quit listening to him. Ra didn't want to lose control. He took revenge on them. He asked the Eye of Ra to turn into a fierce lioness. It began killing everyone.

Both Zeus and Ra have strengths, powers, and weaknesses. Considering everything you just learned, who do *you* think is the stronger god?

Zeus

Ra

ZEUS VS. RA AT A GLANCE

Name:	Zeus
God of:	The sky, lightning, thunder, weather, law, honor, and justice
Appearance:	Zeus has a strong, muscular body and long, curly hair. He usually has a short beard and sometimes wears a crown of oak leaves.
Weapons:	Lightning bolts and thunder
Strengths:	Can control the world with his lightning bolts; is a smart, brave warrior; is the supreme leader in the Greek religion
Powers and abilities:	Controls the weather; controls the movements of the stars, sun, and moon; can shape-shift into anything he wants
Weaknesses:	Women and his inability to be loyal, has a bad temper, can be violent and bullies others
Symbol:	Lightning bolts and eagle

Name:	Ra
God of:	The sun, justice, and creation
Appearance:	Ra has the body of a human with the head of a falcon or hawk. A large solar disk rests on his head, and a cobra wraps around the outer edge of the disk like a crown.
Weapons:	The Eye of Ra and a spear
Strengths:	Provides life, warmth, and growth; can change the seasons; controls the sky, Earth, and underworld; is the supreme leader in the Egyptian religion
Powers and abilities:	Created gods, creatures, and mortals; merges with other gods; can ask the Eye of Ra to do anything he wants
Weaknesses:	Egomaniac, throws temper tantrums when he doesn't get what he wants, can be violent
Symbol:	Sun disk

GLOSSARY

chaos (KAY-os)—complete disorder and confusion

deity (DEE-i-tee)—a god or goddess

egomaniac (ee-goh-MAY-nee-ak)—a selfish person only concerned with their own welfare

immortal (i-MOR-tuhl)—living forever and never dying

merge (MURJ)—join or blend

mortal (MOR-tuhl)—a human who will eventually die

Olympians (uh-LIM-pee-uhns)—the 12 Olympians were the main gods and goddesses in Greek mythology

oracle (OR-uh-kuhl)—a priest or priestess who receives divine messages and gives advice about the future

pantheon (PAN-thee-on)—all the gods of a certain religion

pharaoh (FAIR-oh)—a ruler in ancient Egypt

primeval (prye-MEE-vuhl)—ancient, from the earliest time in history

shape-shift (SHAYP-shift)—the ability to transform oneself into another person, animal, or creature

Titan (TYE-tuhn)—member of the ancient and original family of gods before the Olympians

underworld (UHN-dur-wurld)—the mythical land of the dead

READ MORE

Briggs, Korwin. *Gods and Heroes: Mythology Around the World.* New York: Workman Publishing, 2018.

Honovich, Nancy. *1,000 Facts About Ancient Egypt.* Washington, D.C.: National Geographic, 2019.

Menzies, Jean. *Greek Myths: Meet the Heroes, Gods, and Monsters of Ancient Greece.* New York: DK Publishing, 2020.

INTERNET SITES

Ancient Greece: Zeus
ducksters.com/history/ancient_greece/zeus.php

Greek Myths and Legends
kidsnews.com.au/greek-myths-and-legends/

Ra Sun God
historyforkids.net/ra.html

INDEX

ABOUT THE AUTHOR

Lydia Lukidis is a lover of science, the ocean, and Greek mythology. She's also the author of more than 35 trade and educational books for children, as well as 30 ebooks. Her STEM title, *The Broken Bees' Nest* (Kane Press, 2019), was nominated for a CYBILS Award. Lydia is passionate about fostering a love for literacy with children and offers writing workshops and author visits in elementary schools.